Holidays—Count and Celebrate!

Cinco de Mayo

Count and Celebrate!

Fredrick L. McKissack, Jr. and Lisa Beringer McKissack

Enslow Elementary

an imprint of

Enslow Publishers, Inc.

40 Industrial Road
Box 398
Berkeley Heights, NJ 07922
USA

http://www.enslow.com

*To our friends at Trinity Episcopal Church
who love to celebrate Cinco de Mayo.*

Enslow Elementary, an imprint of Enslow Publishers, Inc.

Enslow Elementary® is a registered trademark of Enslow Publishers, Inc.

Library of Congress Cataloging-in-Publication Data

McKissack, Fredrick, Jr.
    Cinco de Mayo- count and celebrate! / Fredrick L. McKissack, Jr. and Lisa Beringer McKissack.
        p. cm. — (Holidays-count and celebrate!)
    Summary: "Kids count from one to ten as they learn about the history and customs of Cinco de Mayo"—Provided by publisher.
    Includes bibliographical references and index.
    ISBN-13: 978-0-7660-3104-3
    1. Cinco de Mayo (Mexican holiday)—Juvenile literature. 2. Cinco de Mayo, Battle of, Puebla, Mexico, 1862—Juvenile literature. 3. Counting—Juvenile literature. I. McKissack, Lisa Beringer. II. Title.
    F1233.M49 2009
    394.262—dc22
                    2007046812

ISBN-10: 0-7660-3104-7

Printed in the United States of America

10 9 8 7 6 5 4 3 2 1

To Our Readers: We have done our best to make sure all Internet Addresses in this book were active and appropriate when we went to press. However, the author and the publisher have no control over and assume no liability for the material available on those Internet sites or on other Web sites they may link to. Any comments or suggestions can be sent by e-mail to comments@enslow.com or to the address on the back cover.

Every effort has been made to locate all copyright holders of material used in this book. If any errors or omissions have occurred, corrections will be made in future editions of this book.

♻ Enslow Publishers, Inc., is committed to printing our books on recycled paper. The paper in every book contains 10% to 30% post-consumer waste (PCW). The cover board on the outside of each book contains 100% PCW. Our goal is to do our part to help young people and the environment too!

Illustration Credits: © 1999 Artville, LLC., p. 7 (map); Associated Press, pp. 5, 9, 13, 19, 23, 28 (numbers 2, 4), 29 (numbers 7, 9); © Bob Daemmrich/The Image Works, pp. 17, 29 (number 6); © 2008 Jupiterimages Corporation, pp. 8, 30; Shutterstock, pp. 2, 11, 15 (all), 24, 25, 26, 27, 28 (numbers 3, 5), 29 (number 10); © Rick Strange/AA World Travel/Topfoto/The Image Works, pp. 21, 29 (number 8); © Roger-Viollet/The Image Works, pp. 7 (inset), 28 (number 1).

Cover Illustration: Associated Press

Contents

Read About Cinco de Mayo!

Holidays bring family and friends together. People all over the world celebrate different holidays. Cinco de Mayo remembers a battle between the Mexican and French armies. The Mexican army won the battle. Cinco de Mayo means "fifth of May." The holiday celebrates how the Mexican army won its first battle. It fought for its independence.

Mexico—A country in North America, just south of the United States.

Puebla—The city in Mexico where the battle of Cinco de Mayo was fought.

revolt—To turn away from and fight against a leader. On Cinco de Mayo, the people of Mexico fought for freedom.

In Mexico, actors show what might have happened on May 5, 1862.

How many presidents did Mexico have in 1862?
One

Benito Juárez (WAHR-ehz) was **one** president of Mexico. He was president in 1862. He ordered the Mexican army to fight the French army.

Juárez was a good president. He cared about his people. He helped them get their freedom. He also helped them find work.

President Juárez was a Zapotec (zah-puh-TEK) Indian. Before he was president, he went to school and became a lawyer.

Benito Juárez

How many boys are wearing sombreros?
Two

These **two** boys are wearing sombreros. The sombrero (suhm-BREH-roh) is a Mexican hat. It has a big brim. The brim keeps the sun out of your eyes. Sombreros are often made from straw. Sometimes they are made from felt cloth. Farmers and cowboys wear sombreros. They keep the hot sun off of their heads.

During Cinco de Mayo, people enjoy dancing. They may do a special dance around the sombrero. This is called the Mexican Hat Dance.

How many main colors are there on the Mexican flag?
Three

The Mexican flag has **three** colors—green, white, and red. The color green reminds people of the fight for independence. The white stripe is for the main religion of Mexico—Catholicism. The color red is for the people who fought in the battle for freedom.

In the middle of the white stripe is an eagle. It is standing on a prickly pear cactus. It has a snake in its mouth. This is an Aztec Indian symbol. The flag stands for three things. It stands for the fight for freedom, religion, and the Indian heritage of Mexican people.

How many girls dance during a celebration?
Four

These **four** girls are dancing during Cinco de Mayo. There are many Mexican folk dances. A lot of these dances include zapateado (zah-pah-tay-AH-do). Zapateado is movement in a folk dance. It includes stamping your heels on the ground to make a loud noise. It is a kind of tap dance.

How many common foods do you see?

Five

Food is a fun part of many holidays. **Five** foods people eat at Cinco de Mayo parties are tortillas (tohr-TEE-yahs), frijoles (free-HO-layes), tamales (tah-MAH-leys), mole (MOH-ley), and salsa (SAHL-sah). A tortilla is a thin flat bread made from corn or wheat. Tortillas are used to make tacos and chips. Frijole is the Spanish word for bean. Tamales are made from corn and meat. They are cooked inside a corn husk or a banana peel. Mole is a sauce made from chocolate, hot peppers, and spices. Salsa is a sauce made from tomatoes, hot peppers, vegetables, and spices.

tortillas

frijoles

tamales

mole

salsa

How many teens celebrate?
Six

These **six** teens celebrate Cinco de Mayo at a park in Texas. Many celebrations have food, dances, games, and shows.

How many stripes on this piñata?

Seven

This boy is making his own piñata (peen-YAH-tah). He has **seven** layers of paper on it. Piñatas are an important part of many Mexican holidays. Cinco de Mayo parties often have piñatas. Piñatas come in many different shapes and sizes. They are filled with candy and sometimes toys. Children swing at the piñata with a stick. When the stick breaks the piñata, candy falls out onto the floor.

How many members in this mariachi band?

Eight

A mariachi (mahr-ee-AH-chee) band plays music during Cinco de Mayo. This mariachi band has **eight** musicians. Most mariachi bands also have a singer and dancers. One song they play is the Mexican Hat Dance. It is a popular dance in Mexico. Mariachi music is made for dancing! The footwork is fast and loud. People tap their heels and toes on the ground.

How many cannons just fired?
Nine

In Mexico, during Cinco de Mayo, men pretend to fight against the French. These **nine** smoke clouds show that cannons were just fired. Every year, the town of Puebla puts on a pretend war. They remember the day when the Mexican army beat the French army.

1 2

Can you count to ten in Spanish?

1	One	Uno (OO-no)
2	Two	Dos (DOSE)
3	Three	Tres (TRESS)
4	Four	Cuatro (KWA-troh)
5	Five	Cinco (SINK-awe)

6	Six	Seis (SAY-ss)
7	Seven	Siete (see-EH-teh)
8	Eight	Ocho (AWE-choh)
9	Nine	Nueve (noo-EH-veh)
10	Ten	Diez (dee-ESS)

More Information About Cinco de Mayo

Cinco de Mayo is a cultural holiday. That means people who share the same background, like being from Mexico, celebrate the holiday together. People all over Mexico—and people of Mexican heritage—celebrate Cinco de Mayo. Cinco de Mayo remembers the famous Battle of Puebla on May 5, 1862. In this battle, the Mexican army beat the French army.

This was a very big deal. The French army was much bigger than the Mexican army. General Ignacio Zaragoza had a clever plan to win. He put people in different places around Puebla to surprise the French. His plan worked. But the French would not give up. They wanted to control Mexico. For four years after the Battle of Puebla, the Mexican army and people fought the French. Finally, Mexico won. Benito Juárez was reelected president.

The people of Mexico wanted to win very much. Before the French came, Mexico had been ruled by the Spanish. For 300 years, Spain controlled Mexico. After the Spanish left Mexico, France wanted to take over. The Mexican people revolted.

Today, people celebrate Cinco de Mayo to remember the courage and spirit of the Mexican people. Every year, visitors come from all over Mexico to the city of Puebla. People act out the battle. They also celebrate with parades, dances, parties, fireworks, and food.

People from all over the United States take part in Cinco de Mayo. The biggest Cinco de Mayo party in the world is in Los Angeles, California. It was started in 1989. Today, about half a million people come to the parade and party. For many people in the United States, Cinco de Mayo reminds them of other battles people have won. Battles such as the fight for equal treatment for all people in the United States. By taking part in Cinco de Mayo, we celebrate the ideas of determination and freedom.

Count Again!

1		One
2		Two
3		Three
4		Four
5		Five

Count Again!

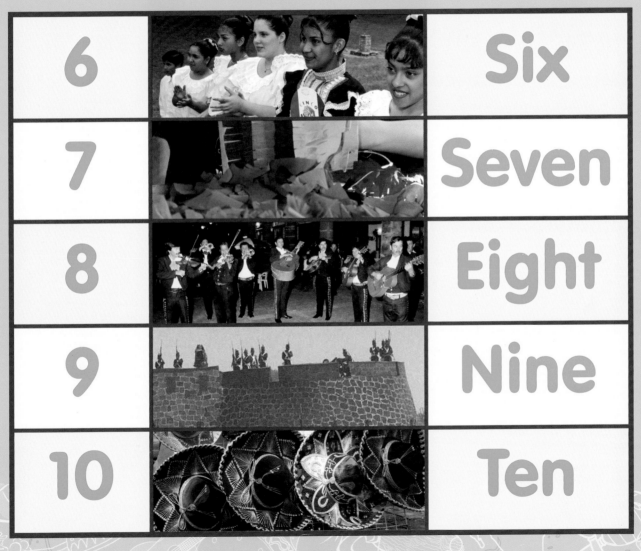

6		Six
7		Seven
8		Eight
9		Nine
10		Ten

Words to Know

army (AHR-mee)—A group of people who fight for a country.

mariachi (mahr-ee-AH-chee)—A group of musicians that play different instruments.

piñata (peen-YAH-tahs)—A decoration filled with toys or candy that is hit with a stick.

sombrero (som-BRAIR-oh)—A wide-brimmed hat worn by Mexican cowboys.

zapateado (zah-pah-tay-AH-do)—A fast, loud tapping of feet during dancing.

Learn More

Books

Krebs, Laurie. *Off We Go to Mexico!: An Adventure in the Sun.* Cambridge, Mass.: Barefoot Books, 2006.

Levy, Janice. *Celebrate! It's Cinco de Mayo!* Morton Grove, Ill.: Albert Whitman, 2007.

Nobleman, Marc Tyler. *Cinco de Mayo.* Minneapolis, Minn.: Compass Point Books, 2005.

Internet Addresses

México for Kids

<http://www.elbalero.gob.mx/index_kids.html>

Mini Sombrero

<http://crafts.kaboose.com/mini-sombrero.html>
Ask an adult to help you make a mini sombrero!

Index